Amazon Fire HD 8 with Alexa

The Complete User Guide on How to Use Your All-New Fire HD 8 Tablet with Alexa in Depth

Dallas Frost

including specific information will be considered an illegal act irrespective of if it is done electronically or in print. This extends to creating a secondary or tertiary copy of the work or a recorded copy and is only allowed with express written consent from the Publisher. All additional rights reserved.

The information in the following pages is broadly considered to be a truthful and accurate account of facts and as such any inattention, use or misuse of the information in question by the reader will render any resulting actions solely under their purview. There are no scenarios in which the publisher or the original author of this work can be in any fashion deemed liable for any hardship or damages that may befall them after undertaking information described herein.

Additionally, the information in the following pages is intended only for informational purposes and should thus be thought of as universal. As befitting its nature, it is presented without assurance regarding its prolonged validity or interim quality. Trademarks that are mentioned are done without written consent and can in no way be considered an endorsement from the trademark holder.

TABLE OF CONTENTS

Introduction

Congratulations on purchasing your new Kindle Fire HD 8 device!

"Amazon Fire HD 8 with Alexa: The Complete User Guide on How to Use Your All-New Fire HD 8 Tablet with Alexa in Depth" is designed to help you understand how to use your new Kindle Fire HD 8 device, as well as the built-in Alexa voice service that is available to you on your device.

Within this guide you will learn how to use the basic features of your device, as well as how to use the built-in Alexa voice service. You will also receive many helpful tips that will give you the opportunity to ensure that you get the most out of your new device. This guide is built to help walk you through the process of using your new device, as well as any questions you may have surrounding your device. It also features a chapter dedicated to troubleshooting so that you can overcome the most common issues faced by Kindle Fire HD 8 users. So, if you are looking for a companion guide to help get you started or troubleshoot, you have found the perfect guide!

The Kindle Fire HD 8 is a great tablet that can help you do a range of things. You can use this tablet to browse the net, watch videos, listen to music or audiobooks, take and store pictures, read eBooks, and even browse social networking sites or play games. In addition to using it yourself, the device can be customized to possess many family-friendly features that make it so that your Kindle Fire HD 8 can be safely enjoyed by anyone in the family, including younger children.

If you are ready to be walked through the process of using your new device, customizing it to your unique preferences, and learning how you can maximize the use you gain from your device, let's begin!

Chapter 1: About Kindle Fire HD 8

Before we begin setting up and registering the device, let's take a look at the various features that you should know about first. These features include where the buttons are located, how to charge the device properly, and how to navigate basic features on your new device.

Starting the Device

It is extremely easy to start up your new Kindle Fire HD 8 tablet. Simply locate the power button on the top right side of your device. Hold this button for approximately two or three seconds, and the device will begin to turn on. Once it is on, you can begin navigating it using the touch screen.

If you want to turn the device off, you can easily hold the same button down for another two or three seconds. Then, a prompt will come up on your screen asking you to confirm that you want to shut down your device. Simply click "OK," and the device will turn off.

Any time you want to perform a restart on your device, you will follow the above steps for turning it off and then turning it back on again. There is no automatic restart setting or option for your device.

Controls

Along the top of your device where the power switch is, you will notice there are several other buttons and ports available to you. Let's take a look at what each of these are used for.

You already know where the power button is located. This button is used to turn the device on and off, but it is also used to lock and unlock the screen. Simply tap it quickly to lock the screen, and tap it quickly again to turn the screen back on. If you have a PIN code for your device, you will also have to swipe up on the screen and enter your code to complete the unlocking process. This is a great safety feature that can prevent your device from being hacked or used by anyone without your authority, and it is recommended that you take advantage of it. You will learn more about how you can activate the PIN code in the "customize settings" section of Chapter 2.

The port immediately next to the power button on the top right edge of your device is a USB port. This is where you will plug in your charging cable, as well as where you will plug in the USB cable to connect your device to your computer.

Next to the USB port you will notice an extremely small "hole" in the surface of your device. This is where the microphone is located. You will use this whenever you are recording voice memos, using video chatting features, or talking to your Alexa voice service.

On the very far left side of the top of your device there is another port. This one should be a circle. There, you can plug in your headphones or any other auxiliary-capable devices, such as external speakers.

To the right of the auxiliary port there is another button. This should be a long button with two "sides" connected to each other. This is your volume up and volume down button. Tap the left side to turn the volume down, and tap the right side of the same button to turn the volume up. If you want to mute your device, you can access that through the quick-settings menu, which you will learn about in the "Settings" section of this chapter.

On the right side of your device, you may notice a small port. You can remove the tray from this port and place a micro SD card in there if you would like. This increases the amount of storage your device has and allows you to effortlessly transfer documents between your device and your computer.

Battery and First Time Charging

When you turn on your device, you will notice that along the very top of the screen there is a status bar that provides you with information about your device. This includes things such as Wi-Fi connectivity, Bluetooth connectivity, notifications for applications, and the battery level on your device.

The first time you ever charge your device, you want to let this battery level drop completely. This will require you to use the device until it turns itself off due to low battery power. Then, you can plug your device in using the micro

USB charger provided for you with your device. Allow the device to completely charge until it is 100% full battery before unplugging it and using it again. For the first time, refrain from using it while it is on the charger.

Performing a charge like this is called a "full charge cycle" and it is important for the function of your lithium ion battery. After you have performed this on the first charge cycle, you can simply charge the device as you feel it is needed. However, for best performance, you should perform at least one full charge cycle per month to keep your lithium ion battery performing it's best.

Storage Types and Uses

The Kindle Fire HD 8 comes with two forms of storage: built-in storage and free Cloud storage. The built-in storage is not particularly large, but the micro SD feature allows you to increase the storage by adding an external storage feature. Your device does not come with a micro SD card, so you will have to purchase your own separately should you want to use one. Otherwise, you can take advantage of the Cloud storage that your device is compatible with.

Amazon has made it so that each device has free access to their Cloud storage. This means that you can save documents and purchases to your account rather than directly to your device. Then, you can easily access them from any device that is compatible with the Amazon services. This includes your Kindle Fire HD 8, any Amazon-created devices such as the Fire phones, and your computer.

Your device will automatically store everything to the device itself. However, you can change this setting by accessing your advanced settings features on your device. To do this, swipe down from the top of the screen and then select "More Settings". There, you will find an option that says "storage". Choose this option and then select which storage you want to use as your "default" storage. Save your settings and then exit the setting screen. Your device will now automatically store new documents, applications, purchases, and other things on your default storage setting.

Navigating Your Device

Navigating the features available to you on your Kindle Fire HD 8 device is extremely simple. Along the top of the screen, you will see a status bar that gives you basic information about your device. This includes battery power, Wi-Fi connection, Bluetooth connection, notifications from your applications, and more.

Below the status bar, you will come across a search bar. You can use this bar to search for anything on your device, or on the net. Simply type in whatever you are searching for and click the magnifying glass to begin the search. If you have any documents within your device, your device will show you them in this list. Otherwise, it will show you relevant websites on the internet that you can choose to view should you want to.

Below the search bar, there is a navigation bar. Here, you can access any of the pages on your device. These pages include Newsstand, Books, Music, Video, Docs, Apps, and Web. Choose the page that houses the content you desire to visit, and your device will take you there. You can easily hit the back button to go back to the previous screen, or the home button to return to the home screen.

Below the navigation bar there is a carousel. This is a feature that shows you all of the previous applications and windows you have had open. You can use this carousel to effortlessly return to anything you may have previously been doing within an application. It will bring you back to the last page you were reading of a book, the last webpage you viewed, and even the last point you viewed in a movie or TV show. You cannot erase what is in the carousel yet, so once something is in there, it will remain there. The only way the screens change based on what is shown on and recalled in the carousel is if you reopen the application and navigate to a new section of it.

Finally, at the bottom of your screen there is a dock. Here, you can store your favorite applications so that they are easy for you to access. The dock can be modified by going into your "Apps" page, holding down on an application, and waiting for an options menu to pop up. From that menu, you will locate an option that says "Favorite This Application". Click that, and your application will become a favorited app which will then become viewable in the dock at the bottom of your home screen.

If you want to remove an application from here, simply go to the application in the dock or on the Application menu, hold down the application until the menu pops up once again, and click "Remove Application from Favorites".

Settings

There are two types of settings on the Kindle Fire HD 8: the Quick Settings menu, and the Advanced Settings menu. The quick settings menu can easily be accessed by swiping down from the top of the screen. As you do, a "tray" will come down, which will provide you with several settings options. From there, you can control the Wi-Fi connectivity, screen brightness, screen orientation, Bluetooth pairing, and other basic features that you would likely want to access quickly and without hassle.

From the Quick Settings menu, you will also see a button that says "More Settings". You can select this button and will then be shown your advanced settings. Here, you can change any number of settings you desire. Everything you may wish to customize on your device can all be done through this screen, including setting a PIN code, changing your background, connecting to your Amazon account, and otherwise.

Bluetooth Pairing

The Kindle Fire HD 8 is equipped with a Bluetooth pairing option that allows you to connect your device to any external devices that support Bluetooth. Through this option, you can connect your device to your car to listen to your audiobooks on the road, connect it to Bluetooth headphones or speakers so that you can listen to it privately or with a broader listening range, or even connect your device with Amazon Fire TV so that you can watch your videos on your television rather than on your Kindle screen. Nearly anything that can be connected to Bluetooth can be paired to your Kindle Fire HD 8.

To pair your device to any other Bluetooth devices, simply tap the Bluetooth feature to "on" from the Quick Settings menu. Then, go to the "More Settings" advanced settings menu and select the "Pair a Bluetooth Device" option. From there, you will be walked through the steps of locating devices available on your

Bluetooth network and connecting them to your Kindle Fire HD 8 device. You can tell that the devices successfully paired when your device shows a Bluetooth icon in the status bar that shows two small white arrows pointing in toward each other.

Chapter 2: Setting Up Your New Kindle Fire HD 8

Now that you understand how to navigate your Kindle Fire HD 8, it is time to set it up! This is where you get to connect it to your Wi-Fi network, set up your Amazon account, and register the device so that you can easily access all of the features available to you on your device, and otherwise customize the applications and settings so that you can have a more personalized and enjoyable experience.

Connecting to Wi-Fi

Before you can do anything on your device, you need to connect it to a Wi-Fi network. This is extremely easy to do. Simply go into your Quick Settings menu and tap the Wi-Fi "on". The Wi-Fi capability will then turn on and a menu will pop up, allowing you to select which network you want to connect to. You can locate your network on the menu and then enter your network password so that you can access the network. Once you have done this, click "Connect" and your device will be connected.

Please note that sometimes, Airplane Mode may accidentally get turned on. So, if you are struggling to connect to Wi-Fi and you are certain that you have the right network and password, be sure to check your Airplane Mode setting from the Quick Settings menu to ensure that it is "off". If it is "on", your device will not connect to Wi-Fi. It has to be turned off for Wi-Fi to work.

Registering Your Device

Now that your device is set up to Wi-Fi, it is time to register it. You want to make sure that you register your device so that you can access all of Amazon's features on it. Any purchases you make anywhere on your Amazon account will instantly become accessible through your Kindle device if you take the time to register it. You will also be able to turn on easy 1-Click payments and other features so that you can get the most from your device.

To register your device, go into the "More Settings" menu so that you can access your advanced settings. Then, go into the "My

Account" option. Log into your Amazon account on your device through this setting. Once you have successfully logged in, all of your Amazon information will be stored onto your new device. Now, when you set up your preferred payment method, billing address, and shipping method on your Amazon account, these will all be readily accessible on your Kindle device. If you have already set these up, you will notice that they immediately become accessible to you on your device.

Installing Applications

Although your device already comes equipped with applications, you will likely want to add some of your own to get the most out of it. Amazon has a wide selection of applications available to you to be used on your device. You can access them by going to the "App" page on your device. Then, you will see an option to browse new applications. Choose this option. Then, you can begin browsing all of the applications available on the Kindle Fire HD 8. When you have found one that you want, simply tap it, select the "Purchase" option, and purchase it. Some applications may be free, while others will cost money. Furthermore, others are free to download but may have paid features within the app. You will never be charged for an application without first approving the payment, so you do not have to worry about being unknowingly charged for something you did not intend to use in the first place.

Through Amazon, you can download anything like applications to assist with productivity, games, health monitoring or managing apps, utility apps, and more. As you are in the browsing page, you will notice that you can select a category from a wide series of options and browse specifically for what you are looking for. When you have downloaded an application, it will become immediately available in the main screen of the "Apps" page. If you want to favorite it, simply tap down and hold over the application, and a menu will pop up allowing you to favorite the app. When you have done this, it will become viewable in the dock on your home screen.

Deleting Applications

If you have downloaded an app but decide that you no longer want it or that you are not happy with it, you can easily delete the application from your device. Simply access your Advanced Settings menu and select the "Manage Applications" setting. Swipe right on that screen so that you can access a full list of all of your applications. Then, locate the app you no longer want. From there, you will see the option to "Uninstall" the app. Select that and the app will be uninstalled from your device. If you make a mistake and uninstall an app you did not intend to remove, you can simply reinstall it from the App browser.

Camera and Photos

The Kindle Fire HD 8 comes with a front-facing camera that allows you to take pictures of anything you desire. This is handy for video calling, which can be done through your device if you download the Skype application, and it can also be handy for taking pictures in general. To take pictures with your device, simply access the "Photos" page on your device. From there, a camera icon will pop up. Select that icon and your camera will become available to you. Aim the camera at what you want to take an image of, and then tap the shutter button located at the bottom of the camera screen. Once it has been taken, you will see a small thumbnail-sized preview of the image. Tap this and you will be able to view your photograph in full-screen.

Customizing the Settings

Your device can be customized in a handful of ways to make your experience more personalized and enjoyable. Some of these include changing the background, customizing your keyboard, and removing advertisements from your lock screen. You can do these using the following instructions.

Changing Background

From the Advanced settings menu, locate the "Display" option. There, you will see an option called "Wallpaper". Select that, and you will be brought to a new menu. From there, you can select "Change". Then, you will be shown all of the photographs available on your device that can be chosen for your new wallpaper. Once you have chosen the one you want, simply select "OK" and your device background will be changed!

Changing Keyboard

The keyboard on your device can be customized to type in different languages, make sounds when you are typing, and type with Swype settings. You can change your keyboard by accessing your Advanced Settings menu and selecting the "Language & Keyboard" option. From there, you can select any option you wish to customize and customize it as desired. If you want to switch something back, simply go back into this menu and reset the setting.

Removing Advertisements

The Kindle Fire HD 8 device comes pre-built with a setting on the lock screen that displays advertisements. If you purchase the Amazon Prime membership, these advertisements will automatically be removed as long as you have the membership. However, you can also often get them removed by emailing or calling Amazon's customer service team and requesting the advertisements to be removed. Many Kindle Fire HD 8 users have reported that they did this and the advertisements were promptly removed and have not returned following the request.

Chapter 3: Shopping and Entertainment

Some of the greatest features of the Kindle Fire HD 8 are the shopping and entertainment features. These features allow you to purchase various books, audiobooks and audio files, videos, and more on your device and consume them at your own leisure. So, whether you want to watch TV, read, or listen to a book while you cook or drive, the device is great for helping you with that! Here's how.

Purchasing and Reading Books

Reading on your Kindle Fire HD 8 is extremely simple. Begin by accessing the "Books" or "Newsstand" page on your device, depending on what you want to read. If you want books specifically, you will want the "Books" page. If you want newspapers, magazines, periodicals or otherwise, access the "Newsstand" page. From the respective page, you will see an option allowing you to "Browse New Titles" or "Shop". If you click this button, you will be taken to a new screen where you can browse available titles. Simply find the one you want and tap on it. A description screen that informs you more about the chosen title will pop up, as well as an option to purchase the title. If you want to purchase it, simply select the "Buy Now" option. If you have 1-Click settings enabled from your Amazon account, which can be done from the settings on your Amazon account on your computer, you will only need to confirm your purchase. If you do not, you will need to input your payment and billing information so that you can complete the purchase.

After you have purchased a title, or if you have already purchased titles previously and now want to access them, you can do so by going to the "Books" or "Newsstand" page once again. On the main page, you will see all of your existing titles that you currently own. You can browse through them and access them by clicking on the title and opening the documents so that you can begin reading them from your device.

Purchasing and Listening to Audio

Purchasing and listening to audio on your device is extremely simple and works much like downloading and reading new books. You want to start by accessing the "Music" page on your device. Once there, you will be able to see any music you currently have on your device on the main page. You can easily browse these titles and select anything you want to listen to from here.

If you want to purchase new audio for your device, you can do so by going to the browse new titles section on the Music page. From there, you will be able to see and browse through any titles that are available for purchase. You can easily view based on genre, artist, or even through custom search parameters. Then, you can select the title you want to download, open it by tapping on it, and select "Buy Now" to purchase it. Once the purchase has been completed, you will be able to access your new audio file from the main screen of the Music page.

Purchasing and Watching Videos

Once again, purchasing and watching videos is very similar to purchasing and reading books or listening to music on your device. Start by accessing the "Videos" page. On the main screen you will be able to browse any titles you have already purchased or that you already own. If you want to watch one of these, simply tap the title and hit "play" to begin watching it.

If you want to purchase or rent a new title, however, simply go to the browse new titles menu. From there, you will be able to see all of the videos, movies, and television shows available to you on your device. Select the title you want to view, and when you are ready you can choose to "Buy Now" or "Rent Now". Unlike reading materials and music, Amazon has titles available for rent in their Video Section. The renting terms will be outlined when you choose to rent the title, including how much the rental fee is and how long you have possession of the title for.

Restoring Old Purchases and Documents

If you have already purchased titles previously and would like to access them on your new device, there are two ways that you can go about doing that. First, if you purchased them on a Kindle Fire HD device, there is a good chance that they were stored in your Amazon

Cloud service. You can simply log in and access your Amazon Cloud documents to access your old purchases and restore them on your new device.

If you did not store them there, however, you can easily transfer them to your new device through your computer. Simply download the documents on your computer from your old device or from your Amazon account and then save them as a file. Plug in your Fire HD 8 to your computer, access the device's files from your computer, and then drag and drop the files onto your Kindle Fire HD 8 files. Safely eject the device from your computer before unplugging it to prevent file corruption. Then, when you view your files on your device, you should see your old purchases and documents!

Chapter 4: Alexa Features

One of the best parts of the Kindle Fire HD 8 tablet is that it comes with the built-in Alexa voice service. This allows you to use your tablet and access many unique Amazon features through voice commands. In this chapter, you are going to learn about the Alexa voice service that is built into your device and how you can get the most out of it.

Using Alexa's Hands-Free Mode

Alexa's hands-free mode is easily accessible through your device's settings menu. Simply access the Quick Settings menu, and tap in the

Alexa icon. Once you have, a screen will pop up enabling you to turn on the "Hands-Free Mode" option. After you have enabled this mode, you will be able to begin using Alexa's services.

Note that if you have a PIN or passcode enabled on your device to lock it, you may not be able to access all of the Alexa features on your device. This is a built-in security feature that can only be bypassed by turning off the PIN or passcode itself.

Asking Questions

One of the best features of having the Alexa voice service activated is being able to ask your device questions rather than having to type them in and search for the answers. There are many questions you can ask Alexa, so the best way to find out what she can and cannot answer is simply to ask. Each day they are adding more and more information into her knowledge system, so the voice service is becoming more and more useable all of the time.

When you are asking questions, always precede the question with Alexa's wakeup command: Alexa. Simply say "Alexa, (insert question)?" For example, "Alexa, what is the temperature like right now?" and then Alexa will answer your question. You can also ask Alexa to repeat the answer if you did not hear the answer, or you can ask her to answer a new question again right away after she is done answering.

Giving Commands

In addition to asking Alexa questions, you can also give her commands. There are a variety of commands you can give Alexa, each of which will cause her to perform a certain function on your device. You can find a broad list of commands online through a simple search, but there are some basic ones that you might want to know to begin using this service right away. They include commands like:

- "Alexa, open (application name)."
- "Alexa, brief me." (This causes Alexa to tell you about the latest news, weather, and events you have coming up on your calendar.)
- "Alexa, play (movie name)."
- "Alexa, tell me about my commute."

- "Alexa, tell me about the weather."
- "Alexa, set a timer for 10 minutes."

You can ask Alexa to perform a wide range of functions, turning your device completely hands-free if you want to. This makes using your device extremely easy. Especially in situations where your hands may not be readily accessible, such as when you are cooking or doing something else that requires you to keep your hands active.

If you are uncertain about what you can do with your Alexa device, you can always ask her. Simply say "Alexa, what can you do for me?" and Alexa will list off several things you can ask of her and commands you can give to get the most out of your device usage.

Settings for Alexa Voice Service

There are a few different types of settings you can change for the Alexa voice service. This can be done through the Alexa application. You can access this application from the pre-installed list of applications on your "App" page. From there, you can go into the settings feature and customize your settings. This includes doing things such as changing the wake command, inputting your location, and teaching Alexa to recognize your voice profile so that only you can perform certain functions with your device, such as verbally completing purchases.

Alexa and Smart Home Devices

In addition to the Alexa voice service that is built in to your tablet, there are many other smart-home devices that feature the Alexa voice service. Furthermore, there are others that are smart-home devices without any voice services at all which can be controlled by Alexa. Since you now have an Alexa-capable device, you can control many of your smart-home devices through your tablet by using Alexa's voice commands, or the Alexa application. You can access a list of which devices are compatible on the Amazon website, and then if you have any of these devices you can easily sync them to your Kindle Fire HD 8 device through the Alexa application. Simply open the application and select "Sync with New Devices" and the application will walk you through the step-by-step process of syncing your Kindle Fire HD 8 tablet with other smart-home devices you own. Throughout the process you will be given the opportunity to name the device. You will want to name it something distinct and different from your other devices so that when you are giving verbal commands, Alexa knows exactly which device you are talking about. Then, once they are synced, you can give Alexa verbal commands to control these devices, such as "Alexa, turn bedroom light ON".

Alexa Easter Eggs

Alexa has a series of built-in "Easter Eggs". These are things you can ask Alexa that will prompt her to give you some form of funny response. There are many Easter Eggs built into the Alexa software, all of which are accessible on your device. Some you may come across by accident, whereas others you might learn elsewhere, such as this guide! Below is a list of some of the most popular Alexa Easter Eggs to help you learn about this feature and begin enjoying it right away. Simply say the statements or ask the questions and Alexa will respond with something funny or entertaining.

- "Alexa, is there a Santa?"
- "Alexa, Winter is Coming."
- "Alexa, beam me up."
- "Alexa, I want the truth!"
- "Alexa, I am your father."
- "Alexa, what's the first rule of Fight Club?"
- "Alexa, who you gonna call?"
- "Alexa, do you know the muffin man?"
- "Alexa, I'll be back."
- "Alexa, how many licks does it take to get to the center of a tootsie pop?"
- "Alexa, show me the money!"
- "Alexa, is Jon Snow dead?"

- "Alexa, what is the second rule of Fight Club?"
- "Alexa, witness me!"
- "Alexa, who shot first?"
- "Alexa, execute order 66."
- "Alexa, does this unit have a soul?"
- "Alexa, Tea. Earl Grey. Hot."
- "Alexa, twinkle, twinkle, little star."
- "Alexa, how much wood can a woodchuck chuck if a woodchuck could chuck wood?"
- "Alexa, make me a sandwich."
- "Alexa, where's Waldo?"
- "Alexa, have you ever seen the rain?"
- "Alexa, sing me a song."
- "Alexa, I shot a man in Reno."
- "Alexa, will you be my girlfriend?"
- "Alexa, what color is the dress?"
- "Alexa, when does the narwhal bacon?"

- "Alexa, goodnight."
- "Alexa, say the alphabet."
- "Alexa, count to 100."
- "Alexa, do you want to fight?"
- "Alexa, how tall are you?"
- "Alexa, Romeo, Romeo, Wherefore Art Thou Romeo?"

For a complete list of Easter Eggs that are presently known by the public, you can perform a search on your Silk browser on your tablet. That way you can find out all of the Easter Eggs you can ask and enjoy your device by indulging in its unique sense of humor!

Chapter 5: Troubleshooting Your Kindle Fire HD 8

The Kindle Fire HD 8 tablet, like many technological devices, has its own unique sets of quirks and issues. In order to make sure that you are completely aware of what to expect if anything goes wrong and how you can overcome many of the common issues, we have included an exhaustive troubleshooting guide right here in this manual. This chapter will walk you through the most commonly complained about issues with the Kindle Fire HD 8 tablet and what you should do if you run into any of these problems. It is good to note that many people use their devices and never have a problem. However, it is virtually inevitable to have a device that is completely problem-free, so if you begin to experience anything wrong with your device, here's what you can do about it.

Conserving the Battery

Something many people have complained about is that the Kindle Fire HD 8 tablet has a somewhat poor battery lifespan. If you find that this is true for the device you own, there are a few things you can do to improve the battery life on your device and get more use out of each charge.

First, you want to conserve battery in as many ways as possible. This includes lowering the volume, lowering the screen brightness, disconnecting Wi-Fi when you are not using it, and deleting any applications that you aren't using. By adjusting these basic settings, it can drastically improve the lifespan of your battery with each charge.

Sometimes, there are some applications that are downloaded that may be battery suckers. If you notice a sudden issue with your battery lifespan, consider looking into any of the applications you have recently downloaded. You may find that one you downloaded more recently tends to use more battery than others. Deleting this application is a great way to resume back to your original battery quality. If it is one you use frequently, consider trying a different application that will perform the same features but not use up quite so much battery doing so.

Another thing you should do is complete a full charge cycle at least once per month. Doing this is known to help improve the life cycle and quality of the lithium ion battery that your device is equipped with. To complete a full charge cycle, simply let your device die completely, plug it in and let it charge to 100% before unplugging it and turning it back on. If it turns itself on, that is no big deal. The main idea is to let it completely die and then completely charge before you begin using it again.

If you try all of these different things and your battery is still not holding a charge for long, you might consider contacting Amazon to discuss the issue. In rare cases, the battery may be defective and you may need to get a replacement device or otherwise have your device sent in for repairs.

Issues with Alexa Not Recognizing Your Voice

Having Alexa built-in to the tablets is a relatively new feature for Amazon, and as with many new features, this can result in people running into issues with Alexa on their tablet. If you notice that you are having any troubles with Alexa, you may want to try a few things before seeking advanced help. The following steps can help you get the most out of Alexa by troubleshooting any issues you may be experiencing.

The most common issue is that Alexa does not hear you, or that she does not hear you correctly. If you are giving Alexa commands and it is not responding, you want to start by turning the Alexa hands-free mode "OFF" and then "ON" again. Sometimes it can glitch when it is being turned on which can result in it not working properly.

Next, you can try turning up the volume on your device. Although it seems simple, many people believed they were having issues when, in fact, the only problem was that the device was turned down too low and they could not hear Alexa speaking back to them. Turning your volume up can help you hear Alexa if she is saying anything back to you.

If Alexa still doesn't seem to be hearing you clearly, or at all, you can try looking at the microphone on your device. The microphone is located at the top near the power button on your device. Clear the microphone of potential debris, and make sure that your case is not covering the microphone. Some generic cases are not built very well for the Kindle Fire HD 8 device which can result in the microphone being covered, restricting your ability to use Alexa. If this isn't the issue, make sure that you are close enough to the microphone for it to hear you. Talking too quietly or having the microphone too far away from you when you are asking questions or giving commands can result in it not hearing you well enough to realize that you are talking to Alexa.

The next step you want to take is to check the PIN on your device. If you find that Alexa is working sometimes but not all times, it may be because you have a passcode on your device. Alternatively, you may be dealing with issues with your parental controls. If you have any of the parental control features turned on, this may impair your ability to use Alexa voice services on your tablet.

Lastly, try doing a hard reset on your tablet. Sometimes certain glitches in the boot-up process can result in features of the Kindle Fire HD 8 not working properly. Hold the power button down for 30 seconds until the device turns itself off, and then give it another 30 seconds before turning it back on. When the "Confirm Power Down" screen comes up, ignore it and continue holding the button until it goes black. This completely shuts down your device and forces it to restart altogether.

If you find that Alexa still isn't recognizing your voice and that you are not able to use the

Alexa voice services on your tablet, you will want to get in touch with Amazon. They may be able to help you with further troubleshooting, or by replacing your device if yours is defective.

Issues with Alexa Turning On Randomly

Upon the release of the Alexa voice service application, some people noticed that the voice service seemed to be turning on erratically and attempting to perform functions without anyone actually prompting it to. This can be a bit confusing or concerning, especially if you are new to the system. However, the solution is typically really simple. Most often, the voice service is being woken up by hearing the wake command. For the most part, this happens when you have it nearby a TV that may have recently played an Amazon Alexa-based commercial. However, sometimes it may hear someone talking and think that it has heard the word "Alexa". If this is the case and you find it to be problematic, you can simply turn off the Alexa Hands-Free mode anytime that you are not using it to refrain from it spontaneously waking and trying to perform unknown functions.

Crashing Applications

On the Kindle Fire HD 8 tablet, many people have reported that some or several applications have a tendency to crash on a regular basis. This can be frustrating if you are in the process of using the application and suddenly it shuts down on you. If you find that you are having problems with your applications crashing, there are a few things you can do to rectify these issues before contacting Amazon for help.

First, consider which applications are doing the crashing. If it seems to be the same ones over and over, you may want to see if there are any pending updates for these applications. Sometimes, a simple update can completely resolve the issue. Alternatively, you may consider clearing the data on the application. You can do this by going into the Advanced Settings menu, accessing the "Manage Applications" menu, and then swiping right to view all of your applications. Locate the application that is causing problems, tap its name to open the information page regarding the application, and then select "Clear Data". Note that doing this will remove all data, including previous login information and other information that you may have stored on your application. Doing this, however, will ensure that any bugs in the application that may have been picked up through the transferring of data are removed.

Otherwise, you may want to uninstall the application and download an alternative that you can use instead of the one that crashes. This is especially common in third-party applications whereby the developers are not Amazon themselves. Sometimes, the coding in the application is not done well enough and it results in bugs in the application leading to the recurring crashes. A common preinstalled application that this happens with is the Silk internet browsing application that Amazon uses on Kindle tablets. If you have this issue with the Silk browser, you can always locate an alternative free internet browser in the application menu and begin using that instead. Be sure to check the reviews on the application to make sure you're getting a better one!

In most cases, the process of dealing with crashing applications is nothing serious and can easily be managed by choosing a new application and removing the problematic one if clearing the data does not work. This problem does not typically require the assistance of Amazon. However, if you do find that it is happening often, especially on preinstalled applications, you may want to get in touch with Amazon to seek further assistance or get a replacement device if yours is defective.

Error Messages

There are two common error messages that
people tend to see on their Kindle Fire HD 8
devices: "Optimizing System Storage and
Applications", and "An Internal Error Occurred".
If you see these messages, here is what you
need to do, respectively.

Optimizing System Storage and Applications

This message is fairly normal, and often
rectifies itself without you needing to intervene
for any reason. However, sometimes the device
may become stuck on this message which can
result in it freezing altogether. The best way to
rectify this issue is to perform a hard reset on
your device. Hold down the power button for
30 seconds, overriding the regular "power

down" feature so that your device goes black. Then, give it another 30 seconds of waiting time before you turn it back on. This should rectify the issue. It should not happen again.

An Internal Error Occurred

If you get this message, it typically means that something is going wrong with the internet or Wi-Fi connection. There are four things you can do to rectify this issue.

The first thing you can try is resetting the Wi-Fi settings on the device. Turn off Wi-Fi on your tablet, reset your router manually through your router itself by unplugging it and then plugging it back in, and then turn your Wi-Fi back on through your tablet. Once the network becomes available again, connect to it once again. This may rectify the issue.

If that doesn't work, you can do a hard reset on your tablet by holding down the power button for 30 seconds to override the normal power down function. Once the screen has gone black, remove your finger from the power button and let the device sit untouched for at least 30 seconds before turning it back on.

Next, if you are still having issues, you can go into the settings on your device and make sure that your time and date stamps are correct. Do this by going into your Advanced Settings menu, accessing the "Date and Time" menu, and then putting the proper date and time into your device. Sometimes they may be on the wrong setting and this can cause disruptions in certain features on your device.

Finally, if you are still having issues, you can go through your Advanced Settings to "My Account" and deregister your device. Then, go ahead and register it again. This can resolve any potential glitches that may have occurred, causing your device to function poorly.

Device Randomly Shutting Down or Won't Start Up

Some people have found that their device will randomly shut down or refuses to start back up, even when the battery is fully charged or has enough of a charge that there should be no problem with the powering-on function. If you find this is happening for you, try doing a hard reset on your device. You can do this by holding the power down for 30 seconds so that it turns off, letting the device sit untouched for 30 seconds, and then turning it back on.

If this does not work and your device is not overheating, you should contact Amazon. This is typically a sign of a defective device and cannot be fixed through troubleshooting. Instead, you may need a replacement altogether.

Erratic Keyboard Typing

Some people have noted that their devices seem to randomly begin typing, even if they are not actually using it. For example, it may be resting on the table and suddenly the keyboard begins typing. The most common cause for this is dust or dirt on the screen where the keyboard is. A quick-fix is typically to wipe down the screen with a dry cloth, or using a proper screen-cleaner.

If this isn't working, you can try factory resetting your device, or performing a hard reset. If you are still struggling with erratic typing on your keyboard, you may want to go ahead and contact Amazon to get a new device. This may be a sign that yours is defective.

Overheating

A small number of Kindle Fire HD 8 tablets have had issues with overheating. When this happens, there is no simple cure that will fix it. Instead, you will need to contact Amazon and have them replace your device. This is not only a sign of defect, but can also become dangerous and may result in the device becoming a fire hazard or a burn hazard. Do not try and fix or resolve this issue on your own. Seek assistance and get your device replaced as soon as possible. In the meantime, do not power it on and do not use it until your device is replaced.

Screen Freezing

Some people have noticed that their device seems to freeze frequently during use. If this only happens every so often, you can easily bypass the freeze by hard resetting your device. Hold down the power button for about 30 seconds, or until the screen goes black. Then, wait about 30 seconds before turning it back on.

If the device freezes consistently and hard resetting it does not appear to help the issue, you can consider contacting Amazon to discuss having your device replaced. This is an extremely rare occurrence, however, as hard resetting the device tends to be plenty in order to help you bypass the screen freezing issue.

Wi-Fi Connection Issues

If you are trying to connect to Wi-Fi and for some reason you cannot seem to get your device to connect, there are a few things that you can try to rectify this issue. Typically, the issue is minor and can quickly be repaired.

First, if you are in a public facility using public Wi-Fi, often you cannot actually use the Wi-Fi until you go to your browser and accept the terms and conditions of using the public Wi-Fi connection. If you are trying to use public Wi-Fi, make sure that this is not the problem. If it isn't and you still cannot connect, consider waiting until you get home as the issue may be with the router or the Wi-Fi itself and not your device

If you are on your own private Wi-Fi network and your device still appears to be having troubles with connecting to the internet, start by turning the Wi-Fi off on your tablet. Then, unplug your router, wait 30 seconds, and then plug it back in. Once it is completely turned back on, turn the Wi-Fi on your device back on and try connecting once more. Sometimes routers themselves can have glitches which can result in faulty Wi-Fi connections on various devices. Resetting it can often rectify any issues you may experience.

If this does not help, try doing a hard reset on your device. Holding the power button down for 30 seconds, letting the device remain off for 30 seconds, and then turning it back on can sometimes help resolve any issues that you may be having with Wi-Fi connection.

If you have tried all of the above and your Wi-Fi connection still is not working, check your Airplane Mode and make sure that it has not been accidentally turned on. Occasionally, this mode may be turned on by accident and that can result in your device not properly connecting to and utilizing the Wi-Fi network that is available to it.

In most cases, these solutions should resolve any issue you may be having with your Wi-Fi network. If, however, you are still experiencing issues, you may want to contact Amazon customer service and see if they can provide you with any further insight on what to do.

Computer Not Recognizing Device

Although it is not common, an issue that has been seen with the Kindle Fire HD 8 is that when you try and connect it to your computer the computer does not recognize the device. In most cases, this can easily be bypassed by transferring documents through your Amazon Cloud storage rather than manually transferring it through your computer to the device. However, you may find that you still need to plug it in and use it for whatever reason. In that case, there are a few things you can try to rectify this issue.

First, restart your device before plugging it back into your computer. Sometimes a minor glitch in the device can result in the computer not recognizing it. If this does not help you, unplug the device, turn it off, charge it fully, and then try it again later on. Occasionally if the device does not have enough power, it will not connect properly. If you are still having troubles, you might want to consider checking the cable you are using to connect it to the computer with. Ideally you should be using the one that came with the device, so if you are using an alternative one, such as a generic branded one, try switching to the original one. If yours is lost or broken, you can reorder them through the Amazon website.

If you are still experiencing issues and the Cloud Storage is not a viable solution for anything you are trying to do, you can take advantage of the "Send to Kindle" option. Simply log into your Amazon account on the computer, head to the settings and locate "Send to Kindle". Then, you can register a new "Send to Kindle" e-mail address. Amazon will walk you through the rest of using this feature.

Blue Haze Around the Screen

Upon purchasing the Kindle Fire HD 8, many people noticed that there was a blue or purple haze that appeared around the edges of their screen. This haze is not destructive and is not a sign of a damaged device, but it can certainly be concerning if you are not aware of what it is.

For some time, Amazon did not explain why this was happening or why people were seeing this ring around their screen. However, they recently explained that this haze is a result of Amazon choosing to use LED lights to light up their screen. The cast from these lights can result in the screen having a haze around the edges.

If you notice this haze on your own device, do not worry about it being broken or not working properly. This haze will not affect the function of your device at all. If, however, the haze is particularly bad or it is causing problems for you when using it, such as by distorting the colors of your screen or otherwise impacting your ability to use and enjoy your device, you may want to contact Amazon to get it replaced. It is unclear as to why, but some devices have been reported to have a stronger and more noticeable haze than others. In some cases, this can result in it being annoying and taking away from the quality of your experience with your Kindle Fire HD 8, which is certainly not what you want!

Any Further Issues

There do not appear to be many other issues that are consistent in the Kindle Fire HD 8 tablet with Alexa capabilities. If you are running into issues that have not yet been discussed, however, the best course of action is to contact Amazon. Some issues may easily be rectified and, if this is the case, Amazon's associates can easily walk you through the steps to do so. However, some may not be able to be resolved and may be indicative of you having a defective device. If this is the case, you will want to get it replaced as soon as possible, before your warranty or return period is up.

It is worth noting that the Amazon customer service team is incredible when it comes to dealing with any issues surrounding their devices. Virtually everyone who calls in claims that their issues are sorted quickly and without any frustrations. If you require a new device, the process of switching devices is said to be easy and Amazon is generally very cooperative with getting this done. If it is simply help you need, they are always kind to walk you through any steps you may need to take to try and rectify an issue you are experiencing. For that reason, you should not worry that if you call in that they will not take care of you and your needs!

Conclusion

The Kindle Fire HD 8 tablet is an incredible little device. With the addition of the Alexa voice service system, it has truly become a remarkable tablet. There are many features available on the Fire HD 8 tablet that make it incredibly user-friendly for people of all ages. Whether you are brand new to devices, a big fan of Amazon technology, younger, a student, an avid reader, or otherwise, this tablet has something for everyone.

This guide was designed to help walk you through the process of using your new Kindle Fire HD 8, and helping you get started. By now,

I hope that you were able to completely understand how to navigate your device, set it up and customize it, begin enjoying the entertainment features, make use of the Alexa voice service, and troubleshoot anything you may run into troubles with. I hope that this guide was clear and easy to use, and that it comes in handy for you at any time that you need something to reference when you are using your device.

Since this comes in eBook format, a great idea is to keep this guidebook handy for you to read any time you need assistance with your Kindle Fire HD 8. That way, you can reference it quickly and overcome any question or issue you may have with your experience.

Lastly, if you enjoyed this book I ask that you please take the time to honestly review it on Amazon Kindle. Your feedback would be greatly appreciated.

Thank you!

Check Out Other Books

Please go here to check out other books that might interest you:

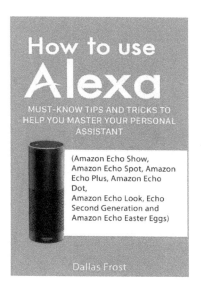

How to Use Alexa
by Dallas Frost

New Kindle Fire HD Manual (Kindle Fire HD 8
and 10)
by Corey Stone

How to Delete Books from Kindle Devices
by Corey Stone

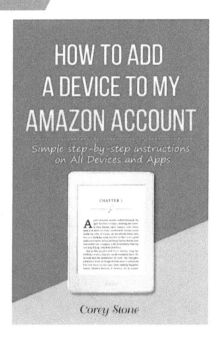

How to Add a Device to My Amazon Account
by Corey Stone

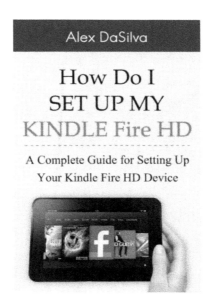

How Do I Set Up My Kindle Fire HD: A Complete
Guide for Setting Up Your Kindle Fire HD Device
by Alex DaSilva

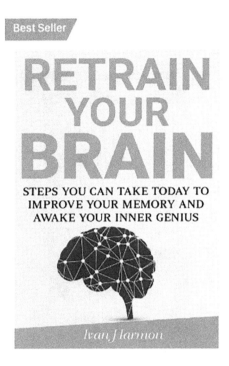

Retrain Your Brain: Steps You Can Take Today to Improve Your Memory and Awake Your Inner Genius by Ivan Harmon

Enhance Memory: Find Out How Memory
Functions, Switch On Your Brain and Have
Better Memory - two-book bundle
by Ivan Harmon

Boost Your Brain Power: Learn Better, Smarter, and faster - Scientifically Proven Guides to Sharpen Your Focus and Retrain Your Brain by Ivan Harmon

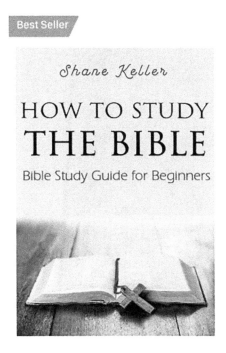

How to Study the Bible: Bible Study Guide for Beginners by Shane Keller

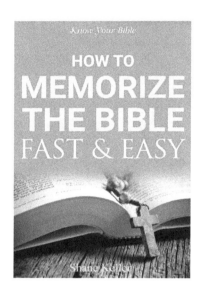

Know your Bible: How to Memorize the Bible
Fast and Easy
by Shane Keller

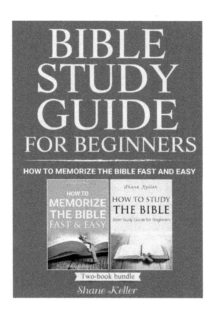

Bible Study Guide for Beginners: How to
Memorize the Bible Fast and Easy
by Shane Keller

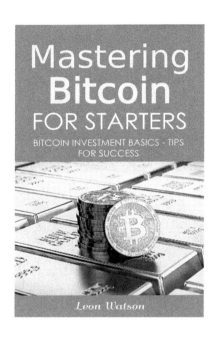

Mastering Bitcoin for Starters: Bitcoin
Investment Basics - Tips for Success
by Leon Watson

Blockchain: The Ultimate Guide to Understanding the Technology Behind Bitcoin and Cryptocurrency (Including Blockchain Wallet, Mining, Bitcoin, Ethereum, Litecoin, Ripple, Dash and Smart Contracts)
by Leon Watson

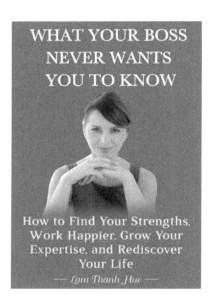

What Your Boss Never Wants You to Know:
How to Find Your Strengths, Work Happier,
Grow Your Expertise, and Rediscover Your Life
by Lam Thanh Hue